GOODBYE MONEY GUILT

SHONA GATES

GOODBYE
MONEY GUILT

Transform your
relationship with money.

CONTENTS

CONTENTS

For every woman out there who dreaded checking her bank account or felt guilty for buying a new bra.

But also for my best friend, lover and partner in crime, my husband Aaron. This book would not be possible without your endless support, enthusiasm, and love.

Thank you for believing in me even more than I do myself.

My legacy,
for Erik, Holly & Hudson
Who inspires me to do better, love bigger, laugh louder
Every day.

CHAPTER

ONE

INTRODUCTION

———————————————

I'm writing this book for you,
For all women,
For our children,
For the next generation.

Why? I was sick of hearing, "I can't afford it" from all the women I knew.

"I'm just not good with money."

"I can't seem to get in front."

"Dealing with money makes me feel sick."

"I'm just not smart enough to make money as she does."

"My husband deals with all of that I wouldn't know where to start."

"I feel so guilty spending anything on myself."

These are the phrases I kept hearing over and over and over again.

At playgroups,
coffee dates,
school drop off,
business events,
meetings,
via messenger, and in phone calls.

With women young and old, no kids and seven kids, from lawyers and financial advisors to stay at home mums from famous influencers to freelancers ... everyone. Hearing beautiful, intelligent, powerful, and confident women that I looked up to still living in fear, scarcity, distrust, and lack of money broke my fucking heart.

It really did.

Because I knew that feeling all too well. Once upon a time, I had let financial stress, lack scarcity, and a poverty mindset absolutely crush the life out of me. Suffocate me and step on my throat every time I tried to move forward in my life. Being broke became my safety blanket, "I can't afford it," use to be my most used phrase. I knew exactly how it felt to be those women; Because I use to be those women, I was those women. No one wins when women live their life in fear of wealth.

And no woman or mum can step fully up into their most creative, expressive, badass joy-filled selves when they are crushed by money guilt and suffocated by scarcity. Mums can't be fully present, mindful and happy when they are terrified to open their bills. Businesswomen can't do their life-changing, impactful, soul-led work when they can only focus on making ends meet.

I want women to be able to step up fully excited and empowered about wealth.

To feel safe, worthy, and deserving of becoming a wealthy woman.

To tap into their daily abundance, that is their birthright.

To be fucking proud of the money, they call into their lives and to spend, earn, and save from a place of over-flow instead of lack.

This IS the mindset and the teachings I pass onto the next generation.

This is my life's work.

And that's why I created my programs, courses, on-line mentoring, and resources to help women step up fully excited and empowered around money.

I do this because every time I hear a woman say, *"I can't afford it,"* my heart breaks.

And I'll keep doing it until the cycle of scarcity and lack is a thing of the past.

If you're ready to break this cycle too ... if you're ready to rise into the abundant babe, you know deep inside your meant to be and do the work to create lasting change.

Then you are in the right place.

So how did I really go from struggling week to week, hiding from my bills, and suffocated by money guilt ... to ABUNDANT AF???

(And don't worry, I'm going to share all about my experience as mayor of struggle town really soon, but now, let me just help set the scene for the work we are about to do.)

Look babe, I wish the answer was a simple one. I could bundle up in a bow and gift you. I wish I could tell you it was some magical formulae, some hidden book a "secret" of sorts. I wish I could tell you, like all the other online coaches in this space, "that a million dollars are only one decision away."

But let's get real...

This work is messy, and it's soul-bearing, it's uncomfortable and digging deep into our subconscious. It's taking a good hard look at your mindset and then challenging and rewriting patterns that have been driving your entire life. Sometimes it happens quickly, and sometimes it takes years of slowly adding in the puzzle pieces until you can see the full picture.

All that I have learned,

The books I have read,

The mentors I have trained with,

The therapy I have done,

The inner work I have journaled.

It has not been easy. There has been no guide, no steps, no method. It's been me digging and digging and digging to find what I needed.

What I share in my courses and online programs is nothing new ... it's really not, and it's probably not "smart" business to share with you. But, the fact is none of the information about manifestation or calling in abundance and wealth is NEW! This information has been around hundreds of years and spoken and re-spoken by thousands of teachers. Anyone who claims to have the "secret" or the "new, only way" is more than likely offering you snake oil at the low price of $2999.

Because here's the deal...

You absolutely can learn it all if you have the time and the determination like I did. You can buy every book, listen to every podcast, research every method of manifestation; you can have the drive to search out the tiny facts, phrases that make all the difference in your journey towards money mindset freedom.

You can do it yourself, But here's the thing, a lot of people just won't. Life gets in the way, it gets too hard, they don't know where to start, someone knocks their confidence, and they struggle to get back up, they lack support, and somehow ... we end up back where we began. Frustrated, broke, and calling the entire idea of manifestation and money mindset *"bullshit."*

Having felt this before and done this before (too many times to count). I decided to provide a different option for the women who were following my transformation. I wrote this book (heavily pregnant, I might add) that I wish had existed when I started tapping into mindset work and manifestation. I took hours, months, and years of confusion, learning, and personal growth, and I put it into a format that I wish had been created for me. I asked myself how I would take someone brand new to this idea and give them the most impactful results in the most digestible and confusion-free way. And then I used that idea to create this book, straightforward and to the point for real-life women, real-life mums ready to transform their relationship with money and un-fuck their finances for good!

I'm not claiming to have the secret or the magic cure. Because that's on you, babe ... it's up to you to take what I teach and do the inner work to make it happen.

But my work is good, like GOOD.

This book is life-changing, and I'm proud AF of it.

And it WILL make simple work of what would usually be years of digging through it by yourself.

It's giving structure to the journey of transforming your relationship with money and creating a new financial reality.

It's support and accountability, then taking ancient terms and ideas, putting them into language that every human can understand.

It's teaching principles that you can implement as a family. It's beginning conversations that put you and your partner on the same page, and it's giving you tools and resources to actually do the things and implement the change you really need to.

It's sharing with you EXACTLY how I had my life-changing shifts,

It's for the woman who is curious about and mindset work. Still, she has no idea where to start, the type of woman ready to act, the kind of woman who knows and understands the responsibility of using the principles I teach to implementing the steps.

It's for a woman who is ready to let go of her excuses is sick and tired of repeating the same old broke story and more than anything ... wants MORE for her family and herself. This book has been a labor of love, joy, passion, and life's work. It is my message, my heart, and soul pouring out my mouth, waiting for the right people to hear the words.

Is that you? Are you the right person reading these right words at the right time. Are you ready to make a change?

Then let's do this ....

CHAPTER

TWO

THE GIFT ...

_____

Free gift for you

Head on over to https://sexyselfish.kartra.com/page/
FuC15 and get instant access to my Abundance Affirmation Meditation.

THE BEGINNING

I grew up in a family that worked hard, saved hard, and made smart choices about money. My parents always lived by a budget, paid off two houses, and were proud of their financial prowess. They taught me so many valuable skills that I use every day; they showed me how to save money. I bought my first nice car at 18 and bought my first property at 19.

They taught me about budgets, credit ratings and made sure I used a credit card correctly; they instilled the importance of investing in my super and having a plan (Important things that are still in my focus today.) And I am so incredibly grateful for all of that

However, I was also taught
"Money doesn't grow on trees."
"You can have money or happiness, not both."

"We need to tighten up the budget again." (after a shopping day)
"I really shouldn't have bought this for myself."
"We don't spend, we save."
"Debt is bad"

Even as a young girl of 5-6, I remember hearing my mum arguing with Telstra each month to get $10 off our bill. I would listen to my father use *"well I support this family"* as financial power over my mother during a time of tension. I would sense the guilt and shame every time my mother bought anything for herself or us, or the sense of fear over the stack of bills on the counter. I would hear the language of *"well you've had fun now it's time to buckle down and be stricter with money"* every time we had a day out or went to the movies. I remember not ever bothering to ask for dance lessons, barbie dolls, or brand label shoes; I knew it wasn't worth it, the feeling of restriction ever present, even in those days.

As I grew older, I realized that my parents had made intelligent financial decisions; we were quite well off because of those decisions. They still are. However, despite being debt-free and having the safety net money in the bank, the atmosphere around money in my life was still TOXIC.

My relationship with money and the energy of wealth

was detrimental, greedy, shameful, guilty, and just downright dirty.

In my late teens, it became even more present, the way I delt with money was so up and down it would leave my physically ill, literally anxiety vomiting in the middle of the night about bills that at the time felt so vast and impossible. Looking back now, it seems crazy; most of the time, I had money to pay the bills. I mean was still living at home and working full time. I had money to burn, and yet the thought of seeing my savings account reduce even slightly would leave me in a week-long panic, hating the world and feeling like life was *"so not fair."*

I'm good at savings, I'm good at a budget, I'm good at restricting (exasperated by my eating disorder too, but that's for another book) basically, give me a set of rules to follow and I'm super good at it.

So yeah, I bought a fancy new car with cash, And yep, at 19 my husband (at the time he was my boyfriend) and I bought our first house. And we grew up; my husband worked his arse off, we started multiple businesses and raised multiple babies (3 rad little humans to be exact)

As a mother, I became hyper-aware of my relationship with money,

As a business owner, it was forced to the forefront of my mind every single day. Some months would be huge amazing, fuck it #treatyoself months, and then the next month; I would feel sick to my stomach terrified of not only making enough money but living in fear of also making too much, pretty fucked up hey.

That's when it started to open my eyes. My relationship with money actually doesn't have anything to do with the money....

I've had $50 in the bank to my name and also $50,000. And guess what, my relationship with money was still toxic.

You know what I realized, you can be good at a budget and still have fucked-up energy around money. You can have nothing in the bank or lots of money in the bank and still have fear surrounding your finances and your future. You can have all the investments in place to retire on a pretty paycheck and be terrified to open your electricity bill.

Your relationship with money has nothing to do with what you earn or how much you save.

Your relationship with money, your money blueprint, the way you interact, view, and feel about money that's what is running the show. And if you can improve your relationship with money, you can totally transform the way you earn, save, spend, and even attract money to your life.

So, after an unfortunate episode in the supermarket where my card got declined trying to buy toilet paper ... (yep to broke to buy toot paper) I decided enough was enough. I was going to transform my relationship with money FOR GOOD. And when I had done it, I was going to share it with all the women I possibly could .... So, we could break the cycle of scarcity once and for all.

I'm proud to say that now instead of toxic guilt, shame, and fear surrounding money in my life, my relationship with money is a complete love story. We are besties, and we take care of each other with gratitude and joy. The best bit about my new relationship with money is that it's coming into my life in more significant amounts than ever.

And now I'm going to show you how to create that too.

CHAPTER

FOUR

NOT SO FAST ...

I wasn't sure if I was going to include this little section, but at the end of the day, I would prefer you are 100% ready for what's about to happen instead of getting two pages in and freaking the fuck out. Because there are a few things, I want to let you know before we dive into the nitty-gritty.

First of all, it's going to get real, as much as I'm trying to inspire and relate to you, holding space for you through this journey. I am also going to push you a little, call you out on your bullshit, and with love, make you honest with yourself.

Because babe, teaching affirmations, journaling prompts, and money rituals, that stuff is easy, that stuff is marketable and sellable.

It's palatable (that's why everyone is doing it)

But I don't want this to be palatable; I was this to be transformative, revolutionary, life-changing, etc. And that means it's going to have to get a little bit uncomfortable before it gets better.

Can you handle that?

Some of the topics we are going to share might be triggering; some of the conversations about subconscious patterns and rewriting your money relationship may bring up a lot of emotions ... and that's ok. It's healthy, it's to be expected, and even though it can feel uncomfortable, it's a fantastic sign that it's working.

Second of all, I want to remind you; I'm not a miracle worker. I can't magically make this all happen for you just because you had the guts to pick up this book; I mean getting started is half the battle, and choosing to buy this book. You are badass, I'm fricken proud of you.

But the real work, the real change, and transformation. Happens between the pages, between when you put down the book and pick it back up again. The real change happens when you give 100% to the exercises in this book and necessarily do the do, calling it into your awareness errry damn day.

It's up to you.

Thirdly, all the stories in this book are real, name, dates, and some personal information has been altered to respect each character's privacy. I wasn't going to include these client stories in this book, I didn't want it to seem like testimonials on a sales page, but I know for a lot of us, stories are how we learn, how we connect and how we can relate these concepts into real-life applications. So, I've decided to add them whenever it would strengthen the message. I hope you get value from these stories, and I thank every client who participated and shared them with me.

So, having said all that now.

let's get started.

DEAR MONEY ...

Before we can rewire your money relationship to get rid of money guilt forever... we first have to acknowledge where we are at with our money relationship right now.

Today. At this moment.

Like in AA and most recovery or 12 step programs, the very first step is always acknowledging where you're at, saying here I am, this is what's going on, and I'm ready to face it head-on.

Enter ... the money letter

The money letter has to be one of the most profound exercises I've done along my development journey. The Money letter was first introduced to me by Molly Sapp. Then backed up by Jen Sincero in her book, *"you are a money-making badass."* The money letter is one of the cornerstone exercises when you start looking at your money relationship, and yet I almost didn't put it in this book. Because you see, it's done... like so overdone.

Every money mindset coach will tell you about it; the thing is, though, it works. It's a powerful AF exercise, and it's key to moving forward into the next chapters, so even though I'm cringing at the thought of re saying what has already been said what feels like a million times. For those of you picking up this book for the first time, reading something on this topic is going to be a game-changer.

For those of you who may have heard of this or maybe done this exercise before, trust me, it's time to look at it again. I write my money letter at least every three months, sometimes more often because it is the perfect way to gauge how you relate to money and what your energy is doing around money.

So, what is a money letter?

A money letter is essentially a letter to money. Duh

The same way you would write to a friend or some-one you know. It's the place where you can be fricken honest about what you feel, what you like, don't like and say all the things you need to say.

Imagine money is a person, and you're going to write them a letter telling them exactly how you feel, but you're probably never going to post it ...You can say whatever you want, feel whatever you want, just get it all out. The money mindset version of Regina George's "burn book" or your high school diary. It's not the stuff your meant to say or should say. It's not the stuff you would write if you knew someone was going to read it. The money letter is all about telling the things you feel you can't say usually. Acknowledging the not so pleasant feelings, we try to push down deep inside or bury away, pretending they don't exist.

It's ok to be angry,
It's ok not to be positive Polly,
It's ok to tell money to go fuck itself,
Let it all out, babe.

I guess the best way to describe it and show you want to do is to share an example.

How about mine?

This excerpt is the very first money letter I wrote back in 2017, copied from my diary ... as you'll see when you read it, my relationship with money was pretty toxic.

16/9/17

Dear Money

I hate you so much, the thought of not having enough of you makes me physically sick. I hate that my life revolves around you and that no matter whether I have a little or you or a lot of you, the anxiety never goes away. This up and down cycle with you is exhausting me ... I can't do it anymore. It's destroying me emotionally and mentally every day. I wish there were more of you in my life. I NEED more of you in my life ... but it seems like the more I need you, the less you are around. I feel like because of you I can't be, do and have the things the real version of me desires, I just get so angry that I need you and so frustrated because I don't know how to get more of you. I don't want to hate you .... But I do, and I want to change that .... But I don't know-how.

Resentfully, Shona

Whew ... reading that and writing that was a lot harder than I expected. Mostly because I've changed so much, I don't even recognize the Shona, who wrote that back in 2017. Looking back on why money found it so hard to come into my life and stay in my life makes sense. I was desperate, clingy, resentful, toxic, and needy

.... Not the type of energy that money wants to be around, but more on that later.

Now it is your turn to write your letter to money. You can do it right here right now. If you aren't able to write it down, simply think about it in detail, write the notes on your phone or do a voice recording, some type of documentation to help you release those feelings. Remember, there is no wrong or write answer, just full-on honesty!

EXERCISE −

If you could speak to money and tell it what you needed to .... What would you say?

Dear Money ....

_____

_____

_____

_____

_____

_____

_____

_____

_____

_____

_____

_____

_____

_____

_____

How did that feel, babe?

Like really, was that super uncomfortable, or did it feel cleansing?

Do you feel slightly lighter, or have you uncovered and recognized that there is a bit of work to do yet?

If it helps you to know, my money letter upgraded, changed, and got a lot more positive, even two weeks after writing this original letter. This exercise is not where you beat yourself up or slip into a guilt cycle. This exercise is just taking a deep breath and acknowledging and accepting where you are right now. This is just right now, tomorrow, the day after, the month after, the year later... will look different. So, let's move forward and write the rest of this story together.

So, let's look at your money letter, what type of language are you using around money?

Even take a highlighter and bring your attention to the phrases you use

Here are some examples from my "dear money' letter.

"I NEED more of you."
"I hate you so much."

"I'm exhausted dealing with you."
"The more I need you, the less you are around."

Look at how desperate, resentful, and angry I sound .... The critical thing here is realizing you are in a relationship with money. If you took these phrases and said them to someone you love and are in a relationship with, how would you feel? There's so much resentment and desperation in my letter, no wonder money didn't want to hang around me, I'm literally repelling it away. Just like if I wrote this same letter to my husband or my friends, they would pack their bags and get out of my life so fast. Because in the real world, no one wants to be around that sad, desperate, angry energy.

As humans, our energy is like a gigantic magnet that attracts or repels the energy we put into the world. Negative thoughts and attitudes attract more negative things, so angry beliefs and attitudes attract more things for us to be mad about, and positive views and opinions attract more positive experiences.

Can you see how your attitude and relationship towards money is possibly poisoning any more money coming into your life?

What energy are you putting out there to the universe? Are you calling in money with appreciation, gratitude, and purpose ... or are you repelling it away with anger, frustration, blame, desperation, and shame?

Like most people at this stage, you probably realize your shitty money story is more of a horror story ???, so how do we change that horror story into a love story?

Gratitude babe ... gratitude!!!

Being intentionally more grateful each day can take a bit of conscious effort at the beginning. However, before you know it, it becomes part of your everyday life. Piece by piece expressing more gratitude and positive energy, calls in more of the things you do want in your life ... like more money, fun, love, and laughter.

My attitude at the beginning of this journey was pretty rubbish. It was a lot of *"it's not fair" "life's out to get me" "nothing I do ever works"* kind of vibe. So, I thought gratitude was a load of bull crap, and yet I knew if things were going to change, I was going to have to change.

So, I began focusing on gratitude by starting a gratitude journal. A $3.00 A6 notebook that I kept next to my bed with a pen, and every night I would write down three things I was grateful for. In the beginning, it was hard. I would stick with the generic, my husband, my kids, my roof over my head. But as the weeks went by, it got easier. I found more things to be grateful for, and I started manifesting more money as a result.

"I am grateful for my electricity bill that gives my power to cook my food and reheat my cold coffee #mumlife."

"I am grateful to pay my car loan because I get to drive my dream car every day."

"I am grateful for my incredible sex god of a husband and the way he kisses me until I melt."

"I am grateful for my children's amazing school that they love going to every day."

Etc etc., you get the idea.

When I "updated" my money story a few weeks later, things had already started to shift in a big way as they will for you in your own time. For me, this updated money letter became my new mantra. I looked at it every day, read it out loud, and occasionally rewrote it until it was my new regular.

Dear money,

I used to hate you so much. I blamed you for everything I didn't like about my life. Now I understand you so much better. You are simply an exchange of energy, not good, bad, or otherwise. You don't control my life anymore, and I know I can always bring more of you into my life if I choose. I know that you want to be a more involved and abundant part of my life. I just have to be open to letting you in and trusting you not to leave me when I need you most. I'm sorry for the way I've treated you in the past, but I promise to be better. Now you excite me, and I am so grateful for all the opportunities and experiences you give me.

Lovingly Shona

Now it's your turn ...

EXERCISE –

If you fully believed and trusted that money could be your best friend and give you all the experiences, opportunities, and things you desire, what would You say to money?

Dear Money ....

_____

_____

_____

_____

_____

_____

_____

_____

_____

_____
_____
_____
_____
_____
_____

Remember to regularly update your money story, nurturing your relationship with money and finances is the key to a healthy fat bank account.

And don't forget gratitude, gratitude, gratitude.

Share how your daily gratitude journaling is making you feel with us. @sexy_selfish

THE BENEFITS OF BEING BROKE ....

Human beings are complicated, intricate, beautiful things. But at the end of the day, we all act out of our self-interest.

Every day we are acting in response to either pleasure or pain. We are either moving away from pain or towards pleasure. Everything we do benefits us in some way. Otherwise, we wouldn't do it. It's against our human nature to act without it helping us somehow, so even the most generous and philanthropic of us, at the core, receive some benefit from our actions.

Whether those actions ease guilt or also aid our feeling of significance is irrelevant. The main point is that even if we think there isn't, there is a benefit to everything we do. Once you can wrap your head around this, a lot of the world seems to make more sense, the way people behave and act even appears to be more understandable.

This concept was hard for me to grasp at first. It wasn't until I was going through treatment for my Eating disorder in 2018 that I finally had a lightbulb moment when it all seemed clear. My incredible, life-changing therapist asked me during one of our sessions to think about what the benefits of my eating disorder were? At first, I thought it was an odd question: I'm sick, miserable, and hate my anorexic behavior; there is absolutely no benefit to it apart from the thinness I thought. My therapist prompted me some more, and then it was like a light bulb went off in my brain.

My anorexia was my safety blanket. It was my way of controlling the world and imposing rules and restrictions so that I felt comfortable. Faced with the abundance of choice in my everyday life around food and feeling unable to navigate those choices, I imposed incredibly strict rituals and rules around food to make me feel comfortable. The hunger pains I experienced every day and saying "no" to food felt like little victories. The benefit was I was duplicating my mother, who I loved, but also dieted consistently throughout my life. I never had to worry about what to have for lunch or what I felt like eating. It was always the game of the fewer calories, the better. It gave me structure and a way to focus my anxiety into something distracting and productive.

There were so many benefits to my eating disorder that I had never realized, I mean they were all stupid, illogical benefits but still benefits nevertheless.

This exercise was the turning point for me in my recovery journey. As I acknowledged these benefits and how illogical and sabotaging they were to say out loud, I was able to release most of them and find strategies to cope with the others. But until I had identified them, it made sense that my eating disorder was so hard to shake. I was holding on so tightly to it because of my subconscious perceived benefits of comfort, familiarity, restriction, and control. Letting go of my eating disorder and moving away from the place of restriction and scarcity to the new unknown world of endless possibilities were terrifying. I had only ever known this version of me, restrictive and controlling ... what did the new abundant me who could eat whatever I felt like even look like? How did I think? how did I make choices etc. etc

It was completely unknown, but I was ready to take that step.

It was also around this time that I started making

links between my dieting history and my restrictive bud-geting history.

I started to realize that restrictive budgets and living paycheck to paycheck gave me the same underlying feelings of comfort and ease in decision making that the anorexia did.Now I understand that seems wholly counter-intuitive and insane, but it's the truth. Like I never had to decide what I felt like eating due to the *"how low can I get my calories"* game, I was using the same tactics with our money. *"I don't have to think about if I want or need something luxurious because when we are broke, all I have to think about is what's the cheapest option/what can we afford."*

Broke was my comfort zone, a super tight budget where we were down to *"can we afford toilet paper"* at the end of each week was my default setting. I could not even imagine how my life would be without restriction, in both money and food. Being broke and having the *"cheapest option/can we afford it/lowest calories"* rule was how I navigated my life, how I made choices, and how I felt safe in the world.

Even though I was creating the vision board, hustling my arse off, saying the affirmations and sticking up my *"check from the universe"* on the back of my toilet door, none of it mattered while I was still committed to the benefits of being broke.

There was an underlying reason behind why I could never seem to crack the next income bracket or save more than X amount in the bank, my subconscious wouldn't let me, and I'm not alone, we all have those underlying subconscious reasons. Sometimes it just takes a simple exercise to bring them forward

So, I want you to take a minute to breathe deep and step into a place of total honestly while you either journal on this or think about it in depth ....

EXERCISE

If I didn't want to make money for some reason, what would it be?

_____
_____
_____
_____
_____
_____
_____
_____
_____
_____
_____
_____

You can use this type of question and answer exercise for different areas of your life, for example, *"if I didn't want to meet the love of my life for some reason, what would it be?" "if I didn't really want that incredible promotion for some reason, what would it be."* You may be surprised by the results, I know I was.

My benefits of being broke extended far beyond the comfort of restriction like I had initially identified. Some of the things that came up for me during this exercise included stuff I'm not proud of, but that I'm going to share with you anyway.

(taken from a journal entry in 2017)
I wouldn't want to make money for some reason because ...???

- *"because my family glorified struggle and working hard."*
- *"because my dad always implied that people who were wealthy had sacrificed their souls."*
- *"because I don't want to push away my family and friends once my lifestyle looks different to theirs."*
- *"I don't want people to expect more of me in terms of gifts of loans financially, I don't want to be used or taken advantage of, and I will find it hard to trust people's intentions."*
- *"I might become, materialistic vain and greedy."*

- *"because I secretly love the adrenaline rush of having to find money, budget and be on top of the bills, etc. it adds drama into the monotony of motherhood and keeps things interesting."*
- *"because I don't feel I'm worthy of the type of financial success I desire, and if it happened to me, I wouldn't even know what to do with it."*
- *"I don't want to be responsible for all the money-making in my family. I'm worried my husband will lose any ambition and drive if he doesn't have financial pressure."*

Your benefits of staying broke might be completely different from mine, or they may be very similar. Still, they all do the same thing; they trick us into self-sabotaging behaviors and pushing money away. Which is the direct opposite of what we want ....

I'm going to spend the next chapter going deeper into rewiring each of these limiting beliefs. But first, I want you to fully understand why they exist, where they come from and why acknowledging and releasing these limiting beliefs is key to transforming your relationship with money and living your most abundant life.

To do that, I need you to understand the conscious and subconscious and the Belief system or blueprint that is running the show ....

I like to think of the conscious and subconscious like an iceberg, a tiny bit poking out of the water, and most of it hiding underneath. The conscious is the part above the water; it's what we can see. In contrast, the subconscious is the big part of the iceberg that is submerged and hidden ... Like how the bottom bit of the ice sunk the Titanic, it's the bottom bit of your subconscious iceberg screwing you over too.

I also like to think of it like a computer keyboard and the program/system that runs the computer. Our consciousness is the keyboard and the mouse. It's the things we have control and intention over. We can move stuff around, create jobs and input data. The subconscious is the background program, the soft wear, the "blueprint" of how the computer works. The subconscious is the rules and how we interpret the data that has been added in.

In a nutshell, the subconscious is running the show.

So, where does our Blueprint/ subconscious programming come from?

Between the ages of 1-7, our brains are little sponges. We are busy observing, learning, watching, experiencing, and soaking up everything around us. After the age of 7, we develop critical thinking, which is where we go, *"Is this true, or is this not."* But up until 7, we can't help but trust the information and experiences we are exposed to. The people in our lives (parents, teachers, aunts, uncles, friends, etc.) plus our environment and skills are all teaching us how to interpret our world. That's where we learn, what's right and wrong, up and down, what feels good and what doesn't, etc. We inherit these beliefs mainly from our parents and so many other experiences, movies, books, society, environment. Sometimes it's hard to pinpoint exactly where they come from, and sometimes it's a mixture of influences.

This blueprint in our subconscious is designed to keep us safe, which was a good thing back when we were cavemen *"don't wander off from the tribe or you'll get squashed by a mammoth"* however not so useful in today's world.

Client example

Sarah worked incredibly hard to build her pottery home goods hobby into a thriving business. She's employed a few staff and now regularly turns over 6 figure years. Yet, she can't seem to grow her savings, and she always feels like money leaves faster than it comes in. When we started working together, we looked at all the experiences around wealth and money from her childhood. Sarah's parents were highly religious and dedicated their lives to serving their church. Her parents

were incredibly proud of the amount of money they donated to their church, even though they both had low-
income jobs. Her parents would continuously look down
upon wealthy people who did not give the same % of
their wages as Sarah's parents did. Sarah and her sisters
hated having to shop at second-hand stores and grew
to resent their parents' dedication to the church. Sarah
vowed to live differently as she grew. She donated money
to causes close to her heart; however, she wishes to enjoy a lifestyle with more opportunities and luxury than
she did growing up.

Sarah's subconscious blueprint was "if you have
wealth, you must give it all away to charity," which she
inherited and interpreted unintentionally from her parent's attitudes and behaviors towards wealth. This subconscious blueprint explained why she felt
uncomfortable accumulating wealth and manifested
bills, impulsive spending habits, and unexpected ex-
penses to remove money from her life. Once we were
able to identify, work through, and release this limiting
belief, Sarah was able to play with the energy of money
and get comfortable with growing her savings.

Can you see how her childhood experiences created
the subconscious blueprint that was self-sabotaging in
her current reality?

These thoughts and views on money are what we aim

to identify, release, and rewrite throughout this book, especially in the next chapter.

LIMITING BELIEFS...

In this chapter, I want to address some of the most common limiting beliefs that I identify in my one-on-one business badassery coaching sessions and my work in the Sexy Selfish Elite membership.

This snapshot is, by all means, not the be-all and end-all compilation of limiting beliefs. There are so many more that I would not have time to teach on in this book. However, this is a start, and these are the most common ones I see, so I decided to address these first.

Some of these you may recognize from your letter to money or benefits of broke exercise, others you may not have already identified, but upon reading, they may resonate deeply within you. This section can be incredibly triggering, so just pay attention to your thoughts and awareness thought this chapter. Some of these limiting beliefs you may want to journal or meditate on in more depth and trust me when I say any feelings of frustration or resentment that come up are healthy, don't worry we will be releasing those feelings in the coming chapters.

Limiting belief, "there's not enough for everyone" "It's going to run out."

I have kept this as a stand-alone limiting belief, but in all honesty, this is the overarching one that weaves its way through everyone we are about to talk about. This is the BIG one ... the one that challenges you to have an entire paradigm shift, so before I begin, I need you to open your mind to the idea that abundance is universal and unlimited.

Many people have what is known as a Scarcity mindset. Sometimes it's called a lack or poverty mindset, or you may find that I've used "my inner broke bitch" term through this book ... but they all mean the same thing.

The scarcity mindset is the belief that there will never be enough, whether its money, food, emotions, or something else wholly. As a result, this guiding belief influences our thoughts, behaviors, feelings, and real-life actions.

Instead of believing and knowing that there is more

than enough for everyone, and there is plenty to go around, you cling to everything you have, hoarding, restricting, needing, out of fear of coming up short.

This mindset can be as small as choosing the home brand strawberry jam, which tastes like plain gelatine over the delicious, however, $3 more expensive jar of organic jam. Or you were replacing a broken appliance. Instead, you duct tape up the wires and continue to use it to save money even though you get a shock 6/10 times you plug it in. For me, it was evident that I would force myself to eat everything on my plate and even finish my kids' leftovers. No matter how full I was or how much I hated doing it, any food left uneaten was *"wasted money."*

Or it can be something big, like not investing in the market, in your business or property because your terrified to lose money, any money at all. It can be denying fun, adventure, and excitement because you are so busy saving for a rainy day, even when that day never comes.

When you have a scarcity mindset, all of your decisions are based on the false belief that there isn't anything else coming that you can't make more money... that you are STUCK.

Have you felt like this before?

This mindset is so damaging for multiple reasons (that we will explore in the coming chapters). But the main point is that it blocks you from seeking new opportunities, and it stops you from growing.

Believing there's *"not enough"* is essentially saying *"this is it, it's as good as it is going to get"* you're putting a lid on your life, your potential, and your finances. It keeps you always focused on keeping what you do have so that you can't see all the fantastic opportunities in front of you. You don't seek opportunities, and you don't want to grow, you stay stuck.

Fear holds us back, keeps us small, and focused on security.

The scarcity mindset also contributes heavily to the feeling of not being worthy of wealth and success. It will amplify your not-enough-ness and can leave you stuck on "just getting by" mode and surviving instead of thriving. You become so stuck in survival mode, making sure you stay afloat and reluctant to take any risks, even when the *"worst-case scenario"*.... Isn't that bad.

Even if we invest a small amount of money, we panic, believing that if we spend it now, we might need it for a bill that will pop up next week.

When we are living our life in scarcity and lack, we

don't make the right decisions. We can't be our most authentic, most joy-filled self, because our choices are coming from a place of fear, not love.

Being stuck in fear manifests in different ways that impact our behavior... For example, we can hide from our money, put off opening our bills, resent checking our accounts. Or it can even ripple out to our relationships, snapping at our kids, pushing people away, resenting your partner for not earning more, etc.

Yet the issues don't magically go away without you addressing them and creating new habits, beliefs, and behaviors. The fear that there won't be enough keeps us in an emotional spiral, where logic can't penetrate. So we need to take a few steps back and look at this logically.

I still remember the dread when the day before payday, our account was at $2.73. The minute I saw my account the negative spiral of thoughts would begin.

"We never have any money."
"I'm so sick of being broke."
"Shit, I shouldn't have got that bottle of wine on Tuesday, we needed the extra money."

*Cue anxiety and vomit-inducing panic and negative self-talk.

But was this self-talk, right? ... not really. It was just my brain clinging onto an idea and running with it.

At the moment, it felt like *"we will never have any money again,"* but the truth was, tomorrow was payday. A few days later, my residual check would come in, and if I wanted to make some more money, I could write a few articles for the blog and get them published today, and the money would hit my account tomorrow.

We can always make more money if we choose. And there is still more money coming.

Take three deep breaths, make them the biggest breaths you have taken ALL DAY!

Now, Repeat after me ...

I CAN MAKE MORE MONEY EVERY DAY IF I CHOOSE
MONEY WANTS TO BE IN MY LIFE
THERE IS ALWAYS MORE THAN ENOUGH

Our thoughts can shift our emotions, and our feelings can change our actions. So YOU are in charge of your reality. Be aware of your thoughts and behaviors, notice when scarcity pops up, or when you make decisions based on fear instead of love... awareness is always the first step to shifting these patterns. Where in life am I acting out of a scarcity mindset?

ACTION STEPS

- Speak your dreams and desires into reality by using the language of abundance instead of scarcity. Instead of saying *I can't afford it,"* shift your thinking and change it to *"I have other priorities right now,"* focus on the abundance you DO have.

- Declutter and cleanse your things. Part of a scarcity mindset is "hoarding"... keeping everything in case one day you might need it again. Let go, donate, give away, or repurpose items that are no longer useful. It's crazy how the more you cleanse and purge items, the wealthier you feel. I genuinely believe abundance and minimalism go hand in hand.

- Avoid comparisons, one of my favorite quotes is *"comparison is the thief of joy"* when we compare our journey to others, let envy, fear, and scarcity guide our decisions and beliefs. It leaves us trying to *"keep up with the Joneses."* Not only will this often leave you with piles of unnecessary and unfulfilling debt ... It keeps us in misalignment because we aren't true to ourselves. Instead, we are adopting other people's goals or ideals of success. Stay in your lane; focus on YOU.

Limiting belief, "Making money is hard."

If the idea of "making money is hard work" was right, it makes sense that the people who work the hardest would be the wealthiest ...??? The plumbers, laborers, stay at home mums to 11 kids, nurses, firefighters, etc. would be the wealthiest in society. However, what we see most of the time, in reality, is the direct opposite.

This calls out the idea that "making money is hard work" as a total and complete lie. And yet this idea is so commonplace now because people feel they can't make money any other way then exchanging their time for an hourly rate. They believe that somehow their boss is in charge of their financial reality and not them, they find the only way to have more money is to work more hours... when this is just not true. Your boss may be in charge of this one stream of income, but studies have shown that the average millionaire earner makes income from at least seven different streams of revenue. And they can still manage time for a beach vacation, watching their favorite show and getting a massage, so you can too.

Once you rewire your thoughts and release the idea that making money has to be hard, new opportunities will open up to you.

When I think about the *"money is hard work,"* limiting belief one particular client comes to mind, and she has permitted me to share a little of her story with you all.

Katie watched her Mother and Father work seven days a week in their grocery store her entire childhood. Throughout her teenage years, she worked in the grocery store as well as a local newsagency, any time she wanted something for herself she was reminded *"money doesn't grow on trees, we work for what we want."* Her parents had an incredible work ethic, something Katie is proud to have inherited from them. Still, she also remembers all the early starts and late nights her parents did running the store, and the only time she saw them relax was on their 2-week river holiday they took every October as a family. *"We have worked so hard this year. We finally deserve a break,"* her father would say.

She was encouraged to study hard, get good grades, and go to university to get a good-paying job, which she did as a counselor. However, her sabotaging behavior started to emerge as her counseling client base expanded. She took on much more work than she could handle, charged much less than she should for her hourly rate, and Even when she had money, she felt guilty. She felt as if she didn't work hard enough, so she pushed herself to do even more. This quickly led to burn out in her mid-twenties.

Katie's childhood experiences created the belief in her subconscious that money can only be earned through hard work, lots of studies, sacrificing A LOT of time, and primarily working till you drop. Eventually, she concluded that working harder may not always be the answer to making more money; that's when she reached out to me.

I worked with Katie to reframe her idea of how money can be made, and she started being inspired in ways she never had before. Her counseling continued to expand, but with healthy boundaries in place, we did the energetic work to be able to raise her prices to a level where they were much more aligned. She even wrote a book about her burnout experience, which now provides her with a passive income stream.

Katie is now pregnant with her first child and looking to step into real estate investing too. She knows that making money can take some consistency and effort, but it can also be made and, most importantly, attracted with ease and flow. The most significant transformation for Katie was when she released the need to feel like she had worked "hard enough" to be deserving of the money she had made. Because really who gets to decide your enough-ness and deservedness except for YOU.

Making money can be hard work, but it can also be easy and fun, depending on what you choose.

You are deserving and worthy of financial abundance just because you are.

ACTION STEPS –

· Research and reframe your idea of how money is made, for example, did you know kids on youtube make thousands of dollars unboxing and reviewing toys? and there are even people out there making money Selling pictures of their feet online ... yes, this is a real thing. Gary Vee's book "crushing it" is fantastic for helping you broaden your idea of how money is made.

· Reality check, the people making the type of

money you would like to make are not necessarily working hard and longer than you. Perhaps they are working smarter, or maybe they have focused on nurturing their relationship with money in the way you are learning to now.

- Use empowering affirmations to rewire your attitude towards money. Katie's favourite assertion during this transition was *"I believe that money comes into my life every day in expected and unexpected ways that are fun and easy, I choose that making money gets to be easy for me."*

Limiting belief, "I'm just no good with money."

This statement is one of the most toxic phrases I hear around money, probably only second to "I can't afford it." It's also one of the most common when I speak to women. How many times have you heard a friend or family member say this? How many times have YOU said it? Too many to count?

Don't worry. You're not alone; in fact, this used to be one of my most used phrases.

You see, I had this belief that I always screwed up with money. Every time I got pocket money as a child, I would either save it for years or excitedly blow it on a new barbie. I'm good at saving money, yet every time I spent the money, even as a child, I would feel this overwhelming shame and guilt. Thus, I began the story that I just wasn't one of those people who was good with money. As I grew up, I started to collect *"evidence"* that I wasn't good with money. That time I lost $50 in the shop, the time I purchased concert tickets one week and then wanted to buy new sneakers the next week, but I didn't have enough, even the time I bought a new car that needed lots of repairs and as my accounts diminished I told myself again *"you are just not good with money."*

This disempowering narrative became my story, and it instantly took me out of the game. It stopped me investing when I could have, it stopped me living life at the moment, going to concerts and traveling when I desired it for fear of mismanaging my money. For a long time, it even stopped me from growing my business and reaching my full financial potential. One of my benefits of being broke and staying small was when I was broke; I didn't have the significant financial responsibility of managing a lot of money.

It's crazy looking back at it. But at the time, my subconscious blueprint was rooted in the feeling of not being able to handle money. I changed this narrative by intention and awareness of my thoughts, forbidding the phrase "I'm not good with money" and recognizing money as a skill.

So, let's get clear .... Being "good" with money is not a skill that some people are born with and some without. Money is a skill, and you can decide not to learn about it not to build a good relationship with it or you can choose to dive into learning, practicing, and getting comfortable with making BULK money.

ITS YOUR CHOICE

No baby is born being able to talk straight away. I've never seen a baby pop out of its mum and go, *"Hi mum and dad, bit chilly out here, any chance I could grab some milk and another blanket."* It just doesn't happen like that. Before the baby can talk, he must first learn to move his tongue, make noises, learn to babble, then eventually mimic sounds, learn the phonics, master a few words, and then put together a sentence. But imagine if the baby got to the phonics step, decided it was a bit challenging, and stopped trying because *"I'm just no good at communicating."* It's the same thing with money. It's not that you will never be good with money, it's just that you need to learn a few more skills first. Oprah, Tony Robbins, Leonard Dicaprio, Warren Buffet, and even Beyonce ... they weren't born with *"financial savviness"* as their personality trait. Like you and I, they had to learn it along the way to where they are today, so don't let the fear of learning, the fear of trying something new, and yes, the fear of possible failure along the way, hold you back.

In the words of the OG money queen Amanda Frances, *"there's no big chalkboard in the sky where some-one has written the rule that you aren't worthy of all the abundance you desire."*

Money is a skill, and there are a million resources out there just waiting to teach you how to master it ... all it takes is a bit of initiative. I often see women come into my programs at a place in their life where they are in debt up to their eyeballs (some even bankrupt), believing that money is *"out to get them."*

After we do the inner work, they leave my programs feeling like a money queen and financial badass.

All because they were ready to let go of the limiting beliefs that were holding them back, and they decided to make money their best friend. Are you prepared to let go of the idea that you are just never going to be good with money?

ACTION STEPS

- Ask your kids if they have learned about a "Growth Mindset" in school … yes, I could dedicate a chapter to teaching you about this, but honestly, a conversation with your little humans about it is going to be so much more powerful. Growth mindset vs. closed mindset is one of the most potent lessons kids are getting in schools today, do some research into it together as a family.

- Dedicate 10 minutes a day, or an hour a week to learn about money, (obviously there are many sexy selfish resources you can access). But also be open to listening to money podcasts, googling budgeting tips, speaking with financial advisors, learning about investing, or even reading some books about wealth. It only takes a few minutes a day, but the more you do it, the more confident you get.

- Check-in with your money. You are never going to be able to grow your wealth or feel more confident with money if you're hiding from it, avoiding it, and neglecting it. It's time to get comfortable with more. Spend 5 minutes every day, checking in with your money. Open your bank accounts (yes, even if it's scary), look at your money, and express gratitude for what you do have. Each day as you do this, your confidence will grow, and the fear and avoidance will diminish.

· The language of *"I'm not good with money"* is now forbidden, swap that disempowering affirmations to something much more exciting and empowering *"I am learning about money"* or *"I am open to new opportunities to become more financially savvy."*

· When you shift your mindset from closed to open, that's when the universe can deliver all the opportunities and abundance to you. You have to be open to receiving it.

· Treat yourself like your child. As a baby, when they are trying to learn to walk but stumble and fall, we don't say *"god you are so shit at this, you should be running already, you are never going to get it, just quit"*.... Instead we say *"You're doing great, try again."*

· Shift your inner dialogue, to encourage yourself as you would your child, *"I love you, and you are enough, you're doing great, let's keep trying."*

Limiting belief, "I'm not ____ enough to deal with money."

You can fill in the blank with whatever you like, smart enough, thin enough, old enough, patient enough, etc. It all boils down to the same idea that you believe you aren't worthy enough or deserving enough to have money and abundance.

It's about worthiness, but it's also about responsibility. In some cases, we decide we are not tall enough, smart enough, confident enough, not born in the right areas, didn't get the proper education, etc. If we blame the outside and the external, we don't have to take responsibility for our current situation.

Babe, it's time to take responsibility, and it's time to decide you are FULLY worthy and FULLY enough.

Meet one of my clients, Alexis. Alexis spent YEARS thinking that success wasn't for her. In her world, living in country NSW, all the successful people she saw where white older men, real-estate investors, car dealership owners, men in agriculture, etc . (don't even get me started on the patriarchy; otherwise this book will be ten volumes) She struggled to find women in positions of power and wealth, let alone young women who liked wearing bright red lipstick and had their septum pierced as she did. Despite not having a lot of examples of young, ambitious women in her life, she still had this deep desire to be successful.

"I'm not confident enough."
"I'm not pushy and masculine enough to be success-ful."
"my style will always stop me from being seen as suc-cessful"

She had these phrases on repeat, and she struggled to grow her VA business.

The blueprint of success in Alexis's mind was entirely male, confident, aggressive, firm handshakes, and deals over beers at the pub. And while this version of success isn't "wrong," it's not the only way. We did need to spend some time expanding her blueprint of success to include some amazing and successful badass women (we did this by reading biographies, following inspiring social media accounts and incorporating her style into a big part of her branding as an online virtual assistant) But underneath all of that, the core part of the problems and limiting belief was that she didn't feel enough, didn't feel worthy enough or deserving enough of success .... All in all, herself worth and self-LOVE was LOW.

So how do we dial up the self-worth, that's the million-dollar question, (literally.)

Now a lot of coaches will tell you, *"just decide it, and it will be true,"* and yes, that is possible. Sometimes just deciding and declaring that as your new normal is enough. But for a lot of us, the imposter syndrome kicks in, and we end up back at square one or feeling even more unworthy.

So, I prefer a build it brick by brick approach. By recognizing your value and the value, you bring to the world every day.

It's a simple exercise, but because it's easy to do, it's also easy not to do, that's why consistency is vital. Experts say it takes 28 days to create a new habit, so I suggest doing this for at least that amount of time, if not longer. At the end of each day, before you go to sleep or while you are doing your gratitude journaling, write down or think of 3 things you value about yourself or three ways you added value to the world today. Sound daunting and scary? Well, that's a pretty good sign that this is EXACTLY the type of transformation you need.

You can even do this with your kids. We do it as a family every night we have dinner, go around the table, share our favourite and least favourite parts of the day and something we did today that made someone smile. Recognize how amazing you are. Realize how important the work you do is to the world. Remember what a badass you are.

Abundance, money, and prosperity do not discriminate. It doesn't care how tall you are if you have red hair or blue if you're shy or confident, male or female, young or old, whether you got an A+ in year 12 science or a D ... it doesn't care. Abundance, money, and prosperity are more significant than that, they are universal, all they care about is your energy, and they want to be in your life.

ACTION STEPS

- Take account every day of the ways you value yourself or how you add value to the world, the worthier, and the more valued you feel, the more abundance you call into your life. #21daysofworthiness

· Remember, no one else in the world gets to decide how worthy you feel, and you are the only person who gets to choose that. The universe only speaks the language of energy, and it doesn't care what you look like, where you are from, or whether you won the softball championship in 2007. Your energy speaks so much louder than any of that.

· Follow and look for successful and abundant humans that you resonate with. My success blueprint for years was a blonde size 0 woman in red bottom heels, so I never felt thin enough, fancy enough, or pretty enough to be successful and wealthy. Once I stumbled across some incredibly successful women on Instagram who, like me, were curvy and wore converses instead of heels, my enough-ness instantly dialed up to 11 .... Because if they were doing it, I finally felt like I could do it too. Redefine your success blueprint by seeking out inspirational and relatable mentors.

Limiting belief, "Rich people are greedy, evil and selfish."

Money is not linked to our morality.

More or less money does not make us good or bad, right or wrong. Those who suffer are not "better," and those with wealth are not "corrupt." And yet, so many of us believe that **"Rich people are greedy, evil and selfish" is** the absolute TRUTH. So, let's take a look at where that belief stemmed from and why it's fiction.

Remember, between the ages of 0-7, we are little sponges, accepting the programming from our environment.

Did you have lots of wealthy affluent people in your life as a youngster, maybe? But maybe not? So, where did we adopt this false "RICH= BAD" mentality? For many of us, it came from the media we were exposed to, movies, books, and television shows that glorified the poor and struggled as "good" and demonized the wealthy, famous, or influential as "bad."

I grew up watching Mean girls, Hating Alison Ashley,

Angus thongs and perfect snogging, The Worst Witch, Sleepover, Wild Child, etc. All fantastic examples of "rich" equal the enemy. As young women, we are so desperate to understand the world around us we turn to things like movies, TV, book, magazines like Cleo, Girlfriend, or cosmopolitan to try and make sense of our society. When every medium is telling you, *"there is always a pretty rich girl who you will dislike,"* you start to create that in your reality. We have been notified and programmed to fit into the stereotypes we are shown. It's disappointing but it happens to so many of us.

I found myself instantly judging those that had more than me, or those I saw as conventionally prettier than me ... without ever bothering to get to know them or give them a chance, they were instantly put in the "enemy" category. As we have all grown up and reconnected, I'm glad to say that some of the girls I classed as "enemy" in high school are now some of my favourite people to connect with. They are all incredibly talented, passionate, funny, kind down to earth women.

We can find the same examples with the wealthy bad guy stereotype in many books and movies. I challenge you now to think about the films and books you read as a child, who was the villain, bad guy, or bully? Was it the rich kid, the corrupt wealthy mayor, the affluent family, the private school bully ???

Can you begin to see where these limiting beliefs are stemming from?

Mr burns from the Simpsons
Malfoy family from Harry Potter
Regina George from Mean Girls
Walter from the Little Rascals
Nanette Manoir From Angela Anaconda
Alison Ashley from Hating Alison Ashley
Miranda Priestly from The Devil Wears Prada
Etc etc

Then as an adult, this belief system is reinforced in every medium we view and are exposed to.

We root for the poor underdogs, and we wait for the wealthy, successful character to be revealed as the shocking, *"I didn't see that coming"* villain.

The way that you think about wealthy, beautiful, successful, and abundant people is helping you to attract more abundance, or it's hindering you and sabotaging you from the inside out.

What's happening is that we are trying to manifest more money on a surface level, we are trying to work on our relationship with money and call more abundance in. We are saying all the affirmations. We are using the "I am" statements. We are nurturing our relationship with money by paying attention to it. However, on a subconscious level, if we believe that rich wealthy, beautiful, affluent people are shitty, evil, greedy, vain, malicious, corrupt, and dirty people, our subconscious is never going to let us achieve what we desire.

That inner seven-year-old that guides our system and runs our emotional programming is the internal decider of right and wrong. And that belief system is telling us that if we become wealthy and abundant will be the wrong person. So, we need to first identify where those messages come from, and then we need to break down each one and ask ourselves, "Is this true."

Because chances are the rich people we see are actually amazing, philanthropic, kind, down to earth humans who worked with passion and integrity to get where they are today. Are there some absolute jerks out there who took advantage. Did the wrong thing and did step on people during their rise to the top? Sure... But it's not everyone. They are the exception, not the rule.

Client Example

Lauren loved spending time with her Aunt Sarah, who was a successful jewelry designer. Aunt Sarah lived in a beautiful townhouse with her partner Ben, choosing to focus on her career instead of having a family. Lauren completely adored her aunt Sarah, her brightly colored nails, convertible sports car, enormous lipstick collection, and getting postcards from all of her Aunts worldly travels. Aunt Sarah would always let her do the fun things, like sneak the Tim Tams, try on all of her beautiful jewelry, drive with her in the sports car with the top down, and Shania twain cranked and even ate popcorn in the guest bed watching movies. However, when Lauren was about 12, her parents had a big falling out with her aunt. A lot of the dinner table conversation centered around how "selfish, greedy and self-centered" Sarah had become. Lauren loved her aunt Sarah, but she loved her parents even more. So, when her parents said "all Sarah cares about is her money, she won't help any of us out, since she became wealthy she's changed, we don't even know her anymore" Lauren believed them.

Wealth became unsafe, selfish, and greedy in Laurens' belief system, even though she was reconciled with Aunt Sarah as an adult. When it came to Lauren's success, no matter how hard she worked, eventually becoming a successful real estate agent for a well-known brand, she still had 0 personal wealth. She desired wealth, growth, and success; however, it always felt just out of reach.

Can you see how Lauren's well-meaning subconscious may be falsely protecting her from losing her parents' love by staying broke and small?

Where is your subconscious trying to protect you?

Remember this; broke people can be arseholes too. Money and wealth are not accurate indicators of goodness.

A broke guy can cheat on an amazing girl.

A wealthy guy can cheat on an amazing girl.

A broke woman can manipulate those around her for her gains.

A wealthy woman can manipulate those around her for her gains.

A broke mum can ignore her child's emotional needs.

A wealthy mum can ignore her child's needs.

Money is not the factor here, so remove the "rich" from the phrase **"Rich people are greedy, evil and selfish."** And it's more accurate. A rewritten expression could be better described as *"some people are greedy, evil and selfish because they don't know better yet"* or better yet *"everyone is doing the absolute best they can."*

Money is only an amplifier and a resource, and it can't change who you really are. If you were vain and proud before you had wealth, you would be those things even more once you have more wealth. If you were compassionate and empathic before you had wealth, you would find those qualities amplified once you have amassed wealth. Money magnifies the impact I can have in this world. It allows me to give back to my community, purchase books to support budding authors, and contribute and invest in start-up companies growing other women's dreams. Money and wealth allow me to give back to charities that are close to my heart, create scholarships for high school students, and provide fantastic opportunities and experiences for my family.

I promise, there is nothing to be afraid of,
The money will amplify the best of you!

Limiting belief, "You can't be successful/rich and a good parent at the same time."

I held onto this belief so tightly, with so much conviction, for so long ... until I was proved WRONG.

Growing up, the real wealthy people I saw and experienced in my life didn't have kids or had private school kids with a party drug habit. (My microscopic country town view I might add). This view led to what I saw as a black and white option. You could either have money or be a good parent ... not both! (so I thought). Watching the OC, Laguna Beach, etc. growing up further cemented this idea. I believed that kids whose parents had money were even more emotionally fucked up than the rest of us. Somehow these thoughts translated in my subconscious too. *"If I work hard and I'm successful, it will mean I have to spend so much time away from my family that my kids will act out to try and get my attention and time." "if I spoil my kids, they will turn into self-entitled lazy turds."*

These beliefs are why I was NEVER really maternal as a child or teenager, I wasn't interested in babies, being a mum, or playing house ... I wanted to play the EMPIRE! I never even saw kids in my future until my boyfriend (now husband) told me two weeks into dating *"I'm in this for marriage and kids, I want to be a dad, so don't waste my time if you don't want that."* We were 17. I knew he would be an amazing dad, and as shocked as I was about how forward he went about it, three kids later and we are happier than ever.

But, for so long, I honestly, completely and 100% believed to my core that I couldn't have it all, that I couldn't have both, that it wasn't even possible.

Until I met millionaires ...who were AMAZING parents.

I don't talk a lot about my network marketing experiences. Many parts of that journey make me cringe with how misaligned and out of integrity I became. But there are also parts of that journey, which made me who I am today. Some of my best friends I met through that journey, lots of life lessons I gained through the personal development and the leadership pathways I was a part of,

And most of all, it exposed me to people that were earning the kind of money, that up until that point I couldn't have even dreamed of.

I sat with multi-millionaires, and we talked about our kids starting school, they had the same concerns I did, will they make friends? will the kids remember to ask if they need to go the toilet? etc

I sat and had lunch with billionaires, who shared how excited they were to become grandparents again.

The money didn't make a difference.

Family was family.

Love was love.

Parents were doing the best that they couldn't, no matter what their bank account looked like.

It prompted me to journal deeper on this, to examples I had in my life of the type of parent I wanted to be and who I looked up to as a mother, As I journaled more and more on this, I realized the VALUES I aspired to embody as a parent and mother would NOT change with wealth. I had friends who lived paycheck to paycheck who's kids always gave them HUGE hugs at the school gate. I had friends who make six figured a MONTH who take their newborn daughter for a walk in her pram every damn day, rain or shine, with their coffee mugs and two dachshund pups, mum and dad, and little Lila walking together ... every day. I knew of other people who worked 70 hour weeks, made a lot of money, and still made time for a bedtime story every night. Despite a crazy work schedule and often being gone before their teenage kids even woke up, I have friends that spend a lot of their day texting hilarious memes to each other in a family chat.

Money was not the factor in "good" parents or "bad."

We are the factor, our values, priorities, intentions, and mindfulness with our children.

ACTION STEPS

- Decide your core parenting values. For example, mine are "honesty, adventure, curiosity, and acceptance." These values will be your true guiding north once you decide what's most important to you, like loyalty, fun, faith, etc. Whether you are broke or abundant, you can cultivate these values for your family and yourself.

- Look at other wealthy, successful people who are great parents, give your mind "proof." Choose this narrative instead.

- Write a list of all the ways you can be more fun, mindful, present parent if you never had to worry about money again. Try and make some of these a reality for you TODAY.

Limiting belief, "all debt is bad."

This belief is so common, its almost pandemic. So buckle up bitches, this chapter is going to get bumpy.

"Debt is bad" was soo wound into who I was, what I believed, and my foundation for everything, that it's been one of my hardest ones to let go of. When your entire belief systems stem from *"debt is bad, so to be a good person, I must have no debt,"* it becomes impossible to reach your benchmark for *"goodness."*

Now does this mean I'm recommending you go out and buy that range rover that's on your dream board because "it's ok, the chick from that book said debt is ok".. umm no, not really. But am I saying we need to check out attitude around debt and create a healthy perspective around it? Yes.

My parents believed in paying off debt as fast as possible, which is impressive, and I'm so glad that they now have a life of freedom and choice without mortgages or car payments hanging over their heads. However, a life without debt isn't realistic for so many of us. And for so long, every time I looked at my "debt" (which was tiny compared to many), I felt like a massive failure.

The more debt I had, the worse I felt,

The worse I felt, the more I struggled to attract, keep, and grow money, so I ended up in more debt, which in turn kept the cycle going. But, slowly, the more I read, the more I learned, the more I tried out new belief systems, I realized that one of the stark differences between broke people and successful, wealthy people was how they viewed debt.

My friends who were worth millions, weren't afraid of debt the way my friends who made 40k a year were.

When I asked my million dollar friends how much debt they were in and if it ever scared them, they told me. *"Shona, its good debt, its debt that makes us money, and if I was ever scared of debt I would never have taken on the debt that allowed us to build what we have today, debt isn't scary or bad, it's the intention of your debt that matters .. you can't grow and be scared of taking risks, it doesn't match up."*

He was right.

Some mentors and money teachers share about "good debt" and "bad debt" good debt being things that make you money and can be considered an asset, like investment properties, business, education loans, etc. The bad debt is defined as anything the opposite of that, a burden that takes money rather than makes money, boats, cars, the home you live in, travel loans, handbags, etc.

This mindset is how the super-rich do it, take $1, figure out how to turn that $1 into 10 ... then scale.

While this is a great way to educate people about different types of debt and encouraging people to collect assets to build their wealth, I do believe labeling debt as "good or bad" can be just as damaging ... it's like how we KNOW that if we label chocolate bars as "bad food"... we want it 100x more than before.

And the more we attach that desperate and forceful energy of "good vs. bad" to money, we are instantly pushing money away from us.

For so long, no matter what I did, my credit card was maxed out. I had read all the finance books, done the budget systems, and was determined to get rid of all my credit card debts for good (because the debt was wrong, right?) Every time I checked my accounts, I felt gross.

Every time I got a credit card statement, I would punish myself by worrying about it for weeks. I would scrimp and save to pay off some of the debt and feel so relieved to see it going down. Yet the next month, the kids would need dental work, our electricity bill would be higher than expected, or my car would need new tires, and suddenly the card was maxed out again.

And so the cycle continued.

The worse my anxiety got. However, the more I dove into my money mindset work. When I started to reframe how I perceived debt (as a choice and a privilege instead of this dirty thing), suddenly, I manifested, out of the blue, the exact amount I needed to pay off the two credit cards and close them FOR GOOD !!!

This belief system that debt is terrible is keeping us small and stuck.

Either in a cycle of accumulating more debt. Or stuck in the same place because we are so scared of having any debt we won't make a temporary sacrifice for a longterm gain.

To move forward and create massive wealth, freedom, and choice, we have to reframe our ideas about debt.

Debt is not the devil.

Paying interest doesn't mean you're an idiot.

Being debt-free isn't everyone's goal, nor should it be.

Debt is not good or bad, and debt is just a choice to pay something off over time instead of upfront.

Let me repeat that for the people in the back ....

Debt is not good or bad, and debt is just a choice to pay something off over time instead of upfront.

With interest, being the energetic exchange for the privilege of paying it off over time.

So let's chat about interest for a minute...

Last year, I got a speeding fine, and yeah, it was unexpected, and it sucked for a minute. I was rushing to pick up a friend because we were headed into a networking event and had a big drive ahead. I didn't want to be late. So I did a 60 in a 50 zone, and four weeks later, I got my fine in the mail.

I sat with it

Accepted the lesson of patience

And paid the fine, vowing not to speed again and thinking I had learned my lesson

It turns out that speeding fine had another lesson to give me. Four months later, I was chatting with my millionaire friend again. He was saying he recently got a speeding penalty in the same spot too. My default response was *"omg it sucks doesn't like it, like I've learned my lesson, but I still didn't like paying for it, hahaha."*

"The price of speed," he exclaimed *"I like going fast sometimes, I can't help it, I guess this is just what I'll pay to go fast."*

I nearly fell off my chair.

A $400 speeding ticket felt HUGE to me. And yet he just saw this as the "price to go fast." After I quizzed him on his mindset around this, I also discovered he's not fussed about pay on time discounts, parking fines, paying extra to get things delivered express, or paying a cancellation fee.

My inner broke bitch was screaming, *"but that's all money you could be saving."* But his attitude toward this was, it's the price for convenience, sometimes fun, and sometimes having what I want now, I'm ok with that. These conversations helped shift things for me, and while I still like my pay on time discounts, I'm determined not to get a parking or speeding fine, and I would never cancel an appointment without as much warning as possible, it made sense.

Interest was like a speeding fine, "the price to go fast."

When it came time to buy my jeep wrangler (my baby and my dream car), we needed to finance a portion of it. My coach at the time (not my current coach) tried to tell me I was crazy for getting finance or even buying a 35k car in the first place ... "the interest," she would exclaim with disgust, shaking her head at me.

She tried to tell me I should not get a five-year loan; instead, I would take the amount the loan would be every month and save that (keeping the car I currently had), and in 5 years, I could buy my jeep with cash. But it just didn't feel right to me, why wait five years when I could have it now and enjoy it over the next five years? When I added up the interest (with making a few extra payments), I would only save $1200 by saving for five years.

$1200 extra in interest, to have a car now, instead of waiting for five years ... uh hell yeah !!!

$1200 was my "price to go fast."

And I tell you what that is a $1200 well spent. I love my car, like LOVE, my car so much. Before Hudson came along, it was my 3rd baby. I love driving it. I love being in it. I love looking at it. This car was my dream since I was 15 and saw the movie Clueless for the first time. And no amount of interest or other people projecting their debt shame onto me could make me feel bad for it.

That's another point I need to share with you. Every single person has their life priorities, experiences, values, and goals. No two people are alike, and yet the world wants to split everything down the middle and go *"these are your wants, and these are your needs"* or "these are good things to spend your money on and these are bad things to spend money on"

But that's just total bullshit !!!

Some people live to travel and see new places, so using an interest-free holiday loan is more of a priority to them than clearing off student debt.

Some people value private schooling, so they will forgo the BMW to make sure their kids get the classes they need to reach their goal and get into law school.

Some people are super insecure about a part of their body, they hate it, it affects their self-esteem, confidence, and dating life, so they use a credit card to get the surgery they have been hoping for, and an entirely new world opens up them.

What I'm trying to say is that there is no "right or wrong" way to spend your life and money. Your priorities are yours alone ... Once you finally stand up and own them, no one else can shame you or project their choices onto you. In a nutshell, it's what I tell my daughter when she wants blond hair instead of her gorgeous auburn locks *"it would be boring if everyone were the same, don't be afraid to own who you are and be different."*

Debt is not good or bad, and debt is just a choice to pay something off over time instead of upfront.

ACTION STEPS

· Get comfortable and bring awareness to any debt you currently have. (we are going to do a forgiveness exercise in the coming chapters, which will help you guilt or shame you are holding onto around debt)

· Express gratitude for your debt. Once upon a time, that debt gave you something great. Whether it was a wonderful vacation, a beautiful wedding day, a medical procedure you needed, paying bills to keep a roof over your head, or investing in your self-growth. Sit with it for a minute and express gratitude for all the experiences, opportunity, and choices that debt gave you.

· Choose to trust that the universe has your back. If you want to remove debt from your life and free up some funds, that's great. But remember, your debt will still hang around unless you increase your overall income and wealth. Rather than restricting to pay off debt (which can result in you still needing loans and credit cards to get by), focus on overflow instead. When I did this, everything changed, and I had the money to pay off my debt in one fell swoop.

· Affirmation *"I am always in overflow, I have more than enough, I have so much money that I pay all my bills and debt off with ease, money is overflowing in my life."*

CHAPTER

EIGHT

FORGIVENESS ....

After the last chapter, you might have a bit of built-up emotion rampaging inside. Sometimes its sadness, guilt, regret but more often than not resentment and frustration. For as many AH-HA moments you might have experienced as you identified the limiting beliefs that might be holding you back, there were probably just as many *"oh FUCK"* moments.

... *"I can't believe my parents fucked me up like this"* is often the response I hear from clients.

But trust me, a parent is never willingly or knowingly going to be like "let give these kids a scarcity mindset" it's just not how humans work. We are all doing the best we can with the information we have. We can choose to break the cycle of scarcity or the pattern of trauma each generation we decide to be better.

I would like to take time in this chapter to help you move through and release any guilt, shame, resentment, anger, disappointment, or feeling of hopelessness when it comes to your limiting beliefs and your money past.

If you are rolling your eyes right now thinking *"here's another self-help bitch, up on her pedestal, talking about forgiveness"* I get it. I was the one rolling my eyes a few years ago. I was a big fan of *"never forgive never forget"* until I realized that holding onto resentment was making me bitter and sending out such negative energy from the universe, all that anger was repelling my abundance.

I was holding onto so many negative emotions; it almost became my safety blanket.

I resented my old MLM mentor for how she cut me out of her life when we left the company. I felt betrayed and worthless.

I was sad and hurt by a group of girlfriends who socially isolated me after my business took off *"your so up yourself,"* they told me.

I was disappointed and frustrated at my family and parents for all the limiting beliefs I had around money.

And I had a HUGE amount of resentment and anger

towards the patriarchy and how women (myself included) were forced to stay small, unseen, unheard vessels.

Not to mention the anger, shame, and self-loathing I had for myself, especially around my past decisions and behaviors with money. Omg, so much money shame. *"You shouldn't have bought that, you're so bad with money, you can't save, you are so greedy,"* etc.

It was only when I honestly sat down with my thoughts and emotions and permitted myself to release them (not to forget them or say that those behaviors were ok) but simply release them. That was when I was able to call in the abundance and success I desired. Because once I let the guilt, anger, and shame go, I was free to call in the good stuff.

I realized holding onto my shame and guilt, my fear and resentment weren't affecting anyone, But for me. To paraphrase Oprah, or someone famous who said a smart thing, holding onto resentment is like YOU drinking poison every day and expecting it to kill the other person. So, take a deep breath, babe, and let's dive into this forgiveness ritual.

FORGIVENESS 101

To make the most of this exercise, it is best to set aside some designated time, find a place you won't be disturbed, and entirely give yourself over to the experience. However, I have also done this in the school parking lot, on the beach, or in the shower at the end of a hectic day.

The time, place, duration, and HOW you do the ritual doesn't matter, your energy and your intention matters.

You need to fully release any lingering resistance and choose to open your heart and your mind to see things differently. We are about to shed your security blanket and the safety of anger. A new lighter freer and more abundant YOU is about to emerge are you ready?

You may like to light a candle, burn some white sage, use some oils of your choice or meditate beforehand. It's totally up to you. Surround yourself with items that make you feel good, wear your favourite comfy track pants, grab your fluffiest cushion, bring your crystals, and make a cup of tea anything that makes you feel good. A journal and pen is a great idea too, or your phone notes if you are not home.

Begin by writing down who you are ready to forgive (and yes, you should include yourself on that list too) include everyone and everything who you feel anger, guilt, sadness, resentment, disappointment, shame, or un de-servingness towards in your past and present. Even doing this can be incredibly cleansing. See how far you can go back. That boy in kindergarten said your ears were big, yep, better add him to the list.

Now comes the bit everyone wishes they could avoid: you need to write down the specific experience you want to forgive and move past. You can include conversations that you need to release and anything that surrounds this particular person or group of people you are ready to forgive. Get detailed about the experience, how did you feel? What did you see? Dive even deep into it, why did it hurt? What was said? Etc. You need to feel it, process it, relieve it, fully and completely. Experience your feelings like a wave, cry, screams, feel what you need to explore, let your body mind and heart ride the wave of your emotion as it begins, peaks and then subsides .... Then we can release it.

What, about this experience, are you ready to release?

I want you to look for the lesson for each person or memory you are now ready to release. What did you learn from this person or experience? The memory may still be painful, but asking yourself for what you learned because of it, can ease the pain by making you grateful for the lesson. What has it taught you?

Now we move to the part of acceptance.

Acceptance doesn't mean condoning or approving someone else's actions. It merely means you recognize your humanity and theirs. You are removing their energetic hold on you. Start by fully accepting anyone involved (yes, this means YOU too) and all the experiences that you have gone through in your life that have led to this current point in time. Remember and recognize that billions of humans are living on a planet billions of years old, and we each have our own story. A story that is as infinitely intricate, complex, and wonderful as yours.

Fully accept YOU and them.

Remember, we only know what we know, and everyone is doing the best they can with the information available to them. No matter what shame, guilt, or perceived lack you have or have experienced ... it's time to accept it all.

Take three deep breaths, with your hand on your heart

You can even affirm to yourself, either out loud or in your head " I deeply accept and love my perfectly imperfect self "

Forgiving ..... read through each memory or person

you are ready to release. Do this one at a time, be patient, take your time, and don't be too harsh on yourself. Acknowledge the bravery it takes to be vulnerable. Go gently. You are safe. Feel it, hold the energy of the person or memory, even if it brings up sadness, anger, or guilt, momentarily hold this feeling.

Now we can release it, take a deep breath and place your hand over your heart, and repeat after me " I am sorry, I forgive you, thank you, I love you." or "I release you from my past, my present and my future self, thank you for the lessons, I release you, and so it is."

Breath deep and repeat this process as many times as you need, feel the heaviness leave your body, your shoulders feel less crunched your chest less tight. Visualize them and the memories floating away from you, fading from view. Cry if you need to trust your body and your heart to process it the way you need it. Release those old beliefs, emotions, and patterns. You are safe.

Keep breathing deep, let the lightness and space in.

Grounding after this type of intense emotional works is essential. However, it looks different for every person. I like to be held, I'm extra cuddly, and I just want to snuggle up with my husband. Sometimes I even feel like I need sex after (which is the ultimate way to ground back into my body) I let myself be vulnerable, whereas other people prefer to be alone. You just need to find a way to come back into your body and ground your emotions again. Some of my clients like to take a bath, a hot shower, maybe have a nap, or make a cup of tea.

Let yourself feel what you need to feel and trust your intuition will guide you moving forward.

Remember, you are loved, safe, supported, and always worthy.

EVIDENCE...

Ok, so far, we have been on a hell of a journey, I'm proud of you girl. Like so proud ... this shit isn't easy breezy cover girl stuff. It is emotional. It is profound and life-changing. Money mindset work is a constant evolution, but the heavy stuff is done for now.

Those that have worked with me closely or are a part of my Sexy Selfish Elite membership know there are many Disney and kid's movie references in my teachings. I can't help it, I'm a mum, and this is how I communicate ideas. So, I want to share with you about the movie "inside out" and how it helped me have a huge light bulb moment regarding "evidence." So, if you haven't seen it, it's pretty cute, you should check it out.

The movie focuses on Riley, a young girl who has just moved to a new city with her parents. We see her view of the world from the outside, but also her emotions (as characters) inside her brain. There is Joy, who is bubbly and effervescent, Sadness who is, well, sad. Plus, Disgust, Fear, and Anger who all trigger a distinct part of her personality. But what hit me like a ton of bricks was the "memory bank."

Every time Riley experiences something in the real world, a message is sent down to the worker bees/ neuron/jelly bean looking characters in the memory bank. They find a corresponding memory and send it back up to HQ, essentially reaffirming patterns.

Now, human brains are designed to find patterns. It's what has ensured our survival, and it's how we understood seasons, the passage of time, which berries are poisonous and which ones aren't, but as vital as it is, sometimes it can backfire on us if left unchecked and unchallenged.

When you think about money, your brain is triggered to collect past "evidence" memories and experiences to learn how to navigate a new situation. So, money might bring up fear, shame, envy, disgust, guilt, anxiety, trauma, feelings of not being safe, whatever it is for you. What I want to do now is create some new evidence for your brain, essentially hacking your mind to KNOW and believe that money gets to be fun, sexy, exciting, and GOOD.

As you are probably feeling lighter and bouncier, so is the tone of this book, it's time to shift gears, challenge those limiting beliefs, and dream a little bigger.

It's time to collect some proof, get your CSI Miami on, and find some evidence of abundance. You get to choose what you believe about money, so first, we must decide how we see wealth. Then we can decide how to feel, believe, act, and think about money moving forward.

This is the moment you say goodbye to the broke bitch version of you and hello abundant AF wealthy woman. The life, success, and abundance you desire ... are possible for you. And as always, this begins with gratitude. Grab a pen and paper or make a mental list of everything you are grateful for right now.

It's such a powerful exercise and Sounds easy, but it's often a lot harder, especially if this is your first time doing something like this. It's so powerful; this is the very first exercise that the women who do my 10-day money babe challenge are tasked with doing. Focus on the prosperity that is already present in your life. Not just money, but in every aspect of your life.

Try to list at least ten things. What feels abundant for you?

_____
_____
_____
_____
_____
_____
_____
_____
_____
_____

I'll give you an example of mine right now ...

I am so grateful for the food in my fridge, fresh organic fruits, and veg that nourish my family and give us energy and pleasure every day.

I am grateful for technology, which allows me to connect with friends, family, and clients worldwide.

I am so grateful for cups of tea in my favourite mug from Kmart, the feeling of the warm cup in my hands and the little ritual of boiling the kettle and steeping the tea makes me mindful and reminds me to be patient.

I am so grateful for my kid's school; its small, friendly and has old school country values like community, inclusiveness, and honesty. I love where we live and that my kids get to go to our little local school.

I am grateful for my sex on legs husband and how he makes me smile, makes me laugh ... and makes me come.

I love coffee ... I mean enough said. I love having money to buy coffee and support my local coffee shops. When I drive to the shop in my jeep and order my coffee (latte one sugar, incase your wondering), I am grateful to the money in my life that allows me to have these choices, opportunities, and experience.

Being honest ... even just sitting at my dining table right now writing that gratitude list has completely shifted my energy, I'm sitting up taller, smiling, and I feel lighter.

Gratitude has POWER.

Early on in my mindset journey, about six years ago, I started a gratitude journal. Keep in mind this was way before you could buy gratitude journals specifically for this purpose and way before it was a cool thing to talk about. I mean people thought I was weird carrying this little notebook around with me (I've shared photos of my battered and well-loved journals over on the Elite membership group) Every night before bed, or during the day as well if I needed a little extra energy shift ... I would grab out my journal and write down at least three things I was grateful for.

I still do this today, and it's become such a big part of my life. We share gratitude at the dinner table at night with the kids "what was the best part of your day today?" and my husband and I share what we appreciate about each other in bed at night before we sleep.

One of the most significant shifts I noticed with my gratitude journaling and expressing appreciation was my relationship with my husband. I would do the dishes every night after dinner (we don't have a dishwasher in this house). The dishes we always a huge sticking point for me, we would finish dinner, he would sit on the couch, I would do the dishes (I hate waking up to a messy kitchen) every night I would slam the plates into the sink, make noise, huff, and puff and resent him for not jumping up to help me. It caused so many arguments over the years, which looking back feels a bit silly. But it honestly really pissed me off. "Just ask me to help," he would say, and if I did ask, he would help, but it was still annoying that he never automatically came to help, that I had to manage and request help ... it drove me nuts.

Occasionally if I were busy with the kids or on the weekend, he would do the dishes without any prompting from anyone. And then be all like *"babe I did the dishes"* proud as punch, probably expecting me to be so thankful, and give him a blow job ... but I would ignore it or be like, "what do you want, a fucking medal? I do them every day" (Yeah old Shona was a bitch about the dishes, not proud of it) But no amount of huffing, puffing, throwing plates in the sink, going on strike, or "asking for help" did the trick .... What did???

Gratitude, which I never expected. I started journaling each night about everything I LOVED and appreciated my husband.

How kind and loyal he is, he will help anyone any time, whether it's changing a tire or helping our daughter holly practice her sight words.

He's so talented and good at what he does, I visit him at work, and I can't even wrap my brain around how intricate and complicated it is. I am in awe of all the knowledge he has

He's an amazing father, pure instinct. He's never read a baby book or a parenting blog, but somehow, he knows exactly how to be the most amazing dad.

The more I celebrated, the good, the more the right parts happened.

I realized what I was doing before wasn't working, and I knew if I wanted the opposite result, I had to do the opposite of what felt natural. So, when he did the dishes or even dried up while I washed, I chose gratitude. I said thank you, and I meant it. I told my husband *"thank you so much, babe, it is heaps faster when you help me, and I get to sit down and relax with you sooner, I appreciate it"* his face lit up …. Lit the FUCK UP !!! Like a puppy or a kid on Christmas morning. Every time he helped or initiated the dishes I did the same, said thank you, and made a big deal about (don't worry sometimes I still felt like, are you shitting me, I do this every day, and you need constant pats on the back) but I kept up with it.

Now I have a man who does the dishes with me every night. I wash, he dries or vice versa. We talk and debrief about our day. I say thank you. He smiles and, all is right in the world.

It was right about the time I was working through this with him that I had the light bulb moment, and I realized I was treating money the same way. Wealth and abundance were in my life, but I was too stuck in *"not good enough what do you want, a fucking medal"* attitude, which pushes money away faster than my husband from a dishcloth.

Gratitude MATTERS. For your relationship and when it comes to money.

Maybe you might like to try keeping a gratitude journal too. Start with an achievable goal. Perhaps you want to write down just one thing you are grateful for every day for 30 days. After that, you might want to increase it. Start with what feels right for you.

Or maybe you want to express more gratitude to those around you.

Right now, I want you to try opening up your banking app on your phone, look at the accounts, and the money you have in them. I know this can feel scary but confront it. Trust me.

Now say thank you, express your gratitude for whatever amounts are in there. It might be $2000, it might be $200, it might be $200, or it might be $2 .... That's ok. The first time I did this exercise, I had $2.73 in my bank account. It was scary, it was confronting, but I expressed gratitude, *" thank you universe for all the money and abundance I have in my life, thank you for all the opportunities, choices and experiences it brings me."*

Immediately after I reframed my energy around my $2.73, I felt better. The crazy thing was, 5 minutes after that, I had a completely unexpected $200 enter my bank account in the form of a bond for my sons' child care from 2 years prior that I had forgotten about.

The universe had my back.

What we focus on and give energy to we attract more of....

So, anger draws more anger,

Positivity attracts more positivity,

Makes sense, right?

GOALS...

The second step to this process is finding evidence of other people living the life and abundance you desire.

Keep intention in mind as I'm sharing this step with you. The key here is to use these people and success stories as inspiration, not judgment or envy.

Judgment and envy put you squarely in the middle of scarity-vill and will make you town mayor of lack (which is the complete opposite of the energy you need to be in to call in more money).

It's easy to see someone who is successful or to do what you desire to do and think *"well, of course, she can do it, but I can't seem to get there"* or *"someone's already doing what I want to do so there's no chance for me"* or even *"good for her, but I'm not ____ enough."*

As you can see from our work in previous chapters, this judgment of people wealthier or more abundant than us can be SOOOO damaging. I can see it now from both sides; my old friends would be like, *" you are so up yourself and absorbed in your business now you're successful."* I would then project that onto other successful women *"of course, Kylie Jenner is successful; she's had it all handed to her on a silver platter."*

Round and round the circles go.

No way sis,
that energy will not fly here anymore.

I had to shift from seeing successful people as threatening and above me to my level and standard.

When we put people up on a pedestal, out of reach, what we are doing is lowering ourselves, and vice versa, when we look down on people, we are doing it because it makes us feel better. That's why we can find ourselves sucked down a wormhole of jerry springer show youtube videos. They subconsciously make us feel better about our situations. (so guilty of this, if anyone wonders why I was late to school on Tuesday) And why some of us spend hours torturing ourselves with #fitspo when we know it makes us just feel awful after it.

Instead, we want to change the energy and intention

.... To look for people to help inspire us and expand our vision as to what is truly possible for us.

For example, I love watching Very Cavalleri (yes, I'm a Laguna beach fan from way back). Seeing what Kristin created with her brand Uncommon James gets me so excited and fired up that I just want to jump on into opening a store. But the biggest thing for me was it normalized her success hard work and abundance. She's a human just like me with 24 hours in her day. She has kids and a husband, a business, employees, and friend drama ... its real life. (Well as real as reality TV gets anyway)

I feel the same way when I watch Chip and Joana Gaines on FIXER UPPER, talk about a fantastic work ethic. Owning a multi-million-dollar brand use to feel totally impossible and far away, now it feels so close I can almost touch it.

You have to find your expanders. Not only is the vibe of women supporting women SO FUCKING POWERFUL, but it's how we all rise together to make abundance passion and wealth, our normal state.

I had this experience again recently, where I was forced to face my limitations and crown one of my friends an expander for me.

It happened when I talked to a friend Natalie about our search for a perfect green piece of land to build a new home. There are about four particular areas I like and one area I LOVE about 30 minutes from where we currently are. Natalie has just built a house out in this area. Of course, she took me on a tour... and of course, I completely drooled over it.

As we sat down to lattes (mine full of sugar, hers with almond milk), she pulled out the phone and showed me the most beautiful properties similar to hers in size and location. Of course, they were beautiful. I dreamily started visualizing myself living there with a long gumtree lined driveway. *"These blocks are so well priced, I can't believe how cheap they are,"* she said to me ...

"cheap," I thought hopefully, and I started to get excited, *"wow, maybe this is possible."* She handed me the phone, and I scrolled down to see the price on one particular parcel of land. That's when it became clear to me that Natalie and I had VERY different ideas about what "cheap" was. Very Very different approaches, her version of cheap was about 3x more than my version.

Natalie's cool though, so when I had to laugh and explain that it was just a tad out of our current budget she was super chill about it, and excitedly started looking at land in one of the other areas (more aligned with my current version of possible) But I couldn't get the difference in our expensive VS cheap ideas out of my head. The more I thought about it, the more I was sure the universe was trying to make me see a lesson. I meditated and journaled on it, asking to see the lesson. My question was unexpectedly answered while I sat in the drive-through, waiting for my coffee.

I realized this experience had shown me two things.

That our versions of what we feel are "expensive" is just showing us our limitations, like the ceiling on what we think we can achieve.

But it also was showing me an expander in my circle. Natalie is entirely comfortable with the idea of a $780,000 piece of land. To her, that type of choice and abundance is a typical, duh, of course, type of vibe. For me, it feels like a stretch; for her, it's an everyday thing.

It's like how other mums lose their freaking mind when they find out I have a cleaner like somehow I don't fit the "millionaire" mold that they think are the only type of people that can afford a cleaner. To them, that's a stretch, but to me, a cleaner is just a regular, duh, of course, type of vibe.

(Guess what guys, cleaners are super affordable, I've had one for four years now, and it costs me just over $75 a fortnight for a full house clean every two weeks. You don't need to be a millionaire to fit it in the budget)

You want to surround yourself with expanders and people who lift you, stretch you, not drag you down, and keep you small.

Look for people who are #goals, who you are inspired by, and who can act as your "expanders." These people represent the wealth, abundance, influence, choice, freedom, and impact you desire. Focus on people who make the type of income you want in a way that feels "normal" and "yeh duh, of course" for them

List some of these people bellow, even include "why" they inspire you, or what you love about them?

_____

_____

_____

_____

_____

_____

_____

_____

_____

_____

_____

_____

_____

A Mentor from my MLM days once told me, *"only take advice or inspiration from people you would be willing to trade places with,"* and I think it's one of my more powerful mantras to remember.

Remember, if it is available for them, it is possible for you too.

CHAPTER

ELEVEN

A NEW REALITY...

In the limiting belief chapters, we identified the things holding you back and pinpointed their origin. Now with all the new evidence we have collected, we get to choose your new beliefs.

This is the exciting bit where you get to write your new future into existence.

How do you feel about money now?

Excited? I sure was when I discovered this kind of work. It was like I found a brand-new door in my house to a secret room I never knew existed. The door had been there all along, but my eyes and mind clouded with anxiety, desperation, and fear couldn't see it. But once I opened that door, my entire world changed.

I guess it is kind of like the red pill blue pill scene in the movie the matrix, and you can either know the truth or stay comfortable in ignorance? The choice is always yours.

So many people do choose to stay in the comfort zone.

Comfortably judging the wealthy, becoming bitter and jealous.

Comfortably hating the government, whining about bills, complaining about taxes.

Comfortably working six days a week for a two week holiday each year, only to come back to work miserable instead of refreshed.

The broke zone might not feel comfortable, but it is the comfort zone in its own way.

But you, You are unique, and we are about to step out of the comfort zone, open the door, and take the pill of truth, NOW, together! So here is the deal, if you do what you have always done you will get what you have always gotten.

… otherwise known as the same + same = same.

You have to decide what you want and then start imbodying your inner version of that NOW. It is consciously recoding your brain and beliefs for wealth. Having Full faith that money wants to be in your life and that the universe fully supports your desires.

At the beginning of this book, you acknowledged your past and present situation with money with a money letter. Now we are going to script the future version of your reality with money because babe, you get to choose what you call in.

Decide it with me ...

If you were to consciously choose that money gets to be easy, fun, and sexy, recoding yourself for prosperity and abundance, knowing that what you wish and believe becomes your reality ... what would you choose?

Write down at least 10 NEW money beliefs ....

_____

_____

_____

_____

_____

_____

_____

_____

_____

_____

_____

_____

_____

Here are some of my personal money beliefs; you might like to use some of these too or create something special to you.

- Money is my best friend and wants to be in my life always.

- Money loves me and loves to be around me, and it is still coming into my life from expected and unexpected ways.

- I manifest money into my life every single day, as if like magic.

- I pay attention to my money. The more I nurture my relationship with money, and the more money comes into my life.

- There is always more money coming into my life. I can choose to make more money whenever I desire.

- I have faith that the universe is here to support my desires, financial or otherwise.

- I choose to know and believe that if the universe closes a door, it just means something even better is waiting for me behind another door.

- I know that I can have whatever I desire, there is no magic rule saying everyone else can have success, but I can't .... I get to have whatever I desire.

- Money is fun, sexy, exciting, and easy for me.

- Money amplifies the best of me and allows me to have a more positive impact on the world

- Money always wants the best for me, and I know the more fun I have, and the more joy I feel, the more easy money comes into my life.

- Money guilt, shame, and fear have no place in my life.

- It is safe for me to be a visibly, wealthy woman in my world.

- I live in a state of abundance, always increasing and expending.

- My desires are enough, just because they are.

- I am enough, just because I am.

- The more money I attract into my life, the more authentic I am, the better mother I am, the more fun partner I am, the more aligned business-woman I am.

- It is my divine birthright to be wealthy and abundant.

These are the new blueprints for your life, and we are adding this coding into your subconscious to become your new regular... Remember, you get to choose.

Come back to these words every day if you can, keep these new beliefs, mantras and blueprints in your mind all day long, the more you repeat them, the more you see them, the more you enforce them, the more they become coded into your subconscious.

I have my money beliefs written and stuck up around my home. On my microwave, in my bathroom, next to my bed, and even as a screen saver on my phone.

Saturate your brain with your new chosen beliefs to make them your reality.

INTEGRATION...

Now we have chosen your new blueprint it's all about integrating and aligning the new version of you into your daily reality. Affirming and keeping the focus on these new beliefs and mantras is the easy bit. But choosing abundance over scarcity in your everyday thoughts and actions, that's what requires some effort and consistency.

This part is ongoing, evolving, and expanding. There is no end or arriving. Like in the journey of life, we continue to grow.

The next stage of your life requires you to choose it consciously. It is about stepping into your higher self, your inner wealthy woman, and the next version of you NOW. And integrating the new abundant beliefs, we have chosen into our everyday life. So, what does that new reality look like to you .... How do those new money beliefs influence your thoughts and actions?

Play with me here and imagine this ...

You get a bill in the mail, old you would have groaned, complained, and shoved it down the bottom of our handbag to be dealt with later (and probably have a panic attack about in a few weeks.) The new you open the bill and smiles, you choose gratitude, and pay the bill straight away, writing thankyou on the bill, even listening in your head all the great experiences you got in exchange for the bills service or product. You smile and move on with your day.

You are at the supermarket in the bread aisle, in front of you are two loaves, one fresh preservative-free and drool-worthy soft, it is $6. The other loaf is the bargain basement option, white, plain, $3. The old you would buy the bargain option, (it's just for the kids' lunches anyway, if it is gross ill just toast it and smother it in honey.) The new you will buy the $6 fresh loaf, of course, who cares if it only lasts two days because it doesn't have preservatives; it's going to be gone by then anyway because it's delicious. The new version of you knows, trusts, and has faith that there is always enough money and that she can still get more if she desires. The new you will drive home, with the smell of fresh warm bread soaking through the car and smiles.

You're on the phone to your mother when you mention signing your daughter on for an intensive gymnastics camp over the school holidays. Your daughter is so excited, and you are so proud of her and her dedication to her training. But your mother starts to give her opinion on what a waste of money it is. The old version of you would instantly get super defensive, offended, and angry. You would start to feel guilty and shameful about investing in the camp and wonder if it is such a good idea when you end the phone call, its tense between your mother and you. The new you can see the situation with a bit of perspective. This is a simple case of your mother's money blueprints and priorities being different (and in this case in opposition) to your money blueprints and priorities. She expresses her concern as any mother would, but you don't have to adopt her money blueprint either. You will stay calm, and move onto another topic of discussion, never questioning what you know is right for you and your family.

It's time to buy a new car, the old you had noticed your reliable vehicle is getting pretty cramped with 3x car seats, prams and a million kid accessories crammed into it. You've resisted for a long time, determined to make it work, even though secretly deep down inside, you lust after a shiny spacious SUV to take the kids to school and back in, you don't feel worthy of something like that. The new you know that it's time to upgrade not only her car but her life. She trusts that there is always enough and knows that a happy mum driving a safer, more spacious vehicle means a happy family. The new you has no issues with debt; she knows that she has simply chosen to pay something off over time instead of upfront, she fully understands the energetic exchange for that convenience. She knows that she is fully worthy enough and deserving of a new car and has faith that investing in a new vehicle will not mean she has to sacrifice anywhere else or prove her enough-ness to get it.

Every day she hops into her new car, it makes her smile.

Energy and intention matters

Your relationship with money matters

And who you surround yourself with matters.

Decide now which old beliefs you are willing to release and let go of, then script and write into reality what you choose to be your new standard moving forward ....

The Situation

The old you would

_____

_____

_____

The new you will

_____

_____

_____

The Situation

The old you would

_____

_____

_____

The new you will

_____

_____

_____

The Situation

The old you would

_____

_____

_____

The new you will

_____

_____

_____

Decide this

Declare it
Step into it every day

Becoming a fully empowered, aligned, and abundant woman doesn't happen because of one big overnight power move. It happens every day in the little moments that we choose love over fear, prosperity over scarcity. And it's all those little moments, choices and decisions that lead us to the BIG change, where we look back on our lives and go *"wow, I did that"*

So, lets' do this.

Do it even though you are scared
Do it even though your heart starts racing
Do it even though you doubt yourself
Do it even though they say you can't

Do it now, with what you have, with where you are ... that's how you begin.

THE NEXT STEP ....

Life is easier with friends and wine.

So is manifesting money. So, let's do it together ...

The point of a mastermind is to get around people who are your kind of people, who like what you like, know about shit you are interested in, and kind of just get YOU!

But maybe and hopefully they have just a little bit more experience actually doing the do... then you do.

Who are maybe just a few steps ahead of you, (which is essential, even though it can feel uncomfortable) because to really and truly up-level into the next version of you, you have to surround yourself with people who inspire and push that growth from you.

The point of the Sexy Selfish Elite Mastermind, specifically, is to step into your next level of abundance ... together.

From a place of totally owning the authentic YOU, connecting with your higher self, and deciding what you are and aren't available for.

Trusting that you CAN have it all, that your desires are enough and that you are worthy of abundance, joy, love, and hell, even multiple orgasms if you desire.

It's all yours.

During 12 months in the Sexy Selfish Elite, you have full access to ME, and my support team. Ask me questions, pick my brains, and let's transform our money mindset and manifest TOGETHER.

I will and do hold total space for you, I created this container to have a place where you can be trusted, cared for, and supported while on this journey. To be surrounded by other women, WHO GET IT!

It might feel scary and now, stepping into it. And yes, it will probably stretch you and ask you to have faith and trust in the universe where maybe you haven't before. But slowly and surely, you will clearly see the self-sabotaging patterns. You will be able to step into a place of more conscious co-creating with the universe and even be ready to face up to your relationship with money head-on. You will be writing new rules, deciding new outcomes, and relaxing into fully trusting the YOU that you are meant to be.

You are meant for more, the fact your reading this email is proof that the desires in your heart are there for a reason.

So, trust in YOU!

Here's what some of the women who have already joined the Sexy Selfish Elite Mastermind with me are saying ...

>>>>>>>

"Shona and the Sexy Selfish Elite is a place that I feel safe and heard and inspired. It picks me up after a bad day and reminds me that the universe answers my order, so I need to be mindful for what I ask for" - Amber

"I Manifested $1500 extra...Struggling week to week doesn't have to be a thing! Rewriting your money story is one thing: learning how to implement

them is another. Plus all the support you could ask for..." - Danielle

"I manifested five new clients this week...I have now got clear on what I want to do with my coaching practice and my life... everything is soo clear now !" - Stacey

"If you aren't doing it, you totally should... Shona has been there for me every step of the way as I grow and become the woman, mother, and business owner I am meant to be" - Sarah.

"I would be so lost without this community.... its become my safe place where I feel totally understood, no judgment, my friends aren't along for the ride on my manifesting and self-growth journey, but I always feel at home with the Elite girls" - Nadia.

" Fridays are my favorite day of the week ... seeing the new sessions and training get uploaded has me feeling all vibey before I've even listened to the best investment I've made I love all the fresh content every week," - Rebecca.

>>>>>>>>

Your life is not a dress rehearsal.

You don't get a re-run.

You can change the direction of your life RIGHT NOW...

If you are tired of struggling financially, or you're tired of having to 'hustle' within your business for clients and cash, And you want to start attracting MORE money $$$ and soul led abundance into your life more easily and effortlessly than ever before... Then this is YOUR time, so start now.

Or you could just sit back, turn on Netflix or scroll Facebook some more...And stay the same person for the rest of your life.

*YAWN

I don't think you want to do that, or you wouldn't have read this far. HELLO, you just read an entire book on this topic, I know you have to lady balls to do this.

Now that you have the facts, it's time to make a choice, either way. It is fine with me....

It's time to decide if being a part of the Sexy Selfish Elite is right for you.

VISIT THIS LINK TO LEARN MORE
www.sexyselfish.com

x Shona

SHONA GATES, IS A MUM OF 3 FROM AUSTRALIA.

Self-proclaimed badass wine lover and authenticity am-
bassador.

Shona is Passionate about helping Mums overcome their limiting beliefs about money, totally transform their Money
Mindset and Un-complicate their finances
Giving them the tools and support to Empower Mums who
want to learn how to manifest Wealth ... without all the fluff.

COACH . AUTHOR . SPEAKER

www.sexyselfish.com
@sexy_selfish

Aligned + Abundant Bundle

TThe Aligned + Abundant Bundle is for women who're ready for the next level of INCONE + IMPACT in their business and lives. This instant access kick up the butt bundle is my favourite and most listened to, most life changing audio trainings, with my most " wow omg shona this is incredible" new ebook and all my other favourite goodies

Basically its all the good things ... for the women who are like "GIVE ME ALL THE THINGS" Does that sound like you ?

1-on-1 Strategy Session

This is the kind of intensive coaching for the woman who has already been working on her mindset. She knows her shit, and she knows that if other women can be successful and achieving similar goals around her then she can too... she's just lacking that next step. Maybe its the strategy, maybe its that success mindset, maybe its even working through some of those pesky money blocks, but either way she's willing ready and excited to go from where she is now to where she wants to be.Thats where I come in. , A powerful conversation, some brutal honesty, a sprinkle of strategy and a total kick start.

Elite Membership

The Sexy Selfish Elite membership is the place for mums who want more,A fiercely supportive girl gang focused on unlocking the best version of themselves and calling abundance on every freakin level. Get full access each month to our knowledge portal, workbooks, meditations, and join Shona and the Sexy Selfish Elite team each month for LIVE Q+A sessions, weekly audio trainings, weekly journaling prompts plus special guest speakers ... and so much more.

Learn more at www.sexyselfish.com

Lightning Source UK Ltd.
Milton Keynes UK
UKHW020105170223
417112UK00010B/1249